Volume 5

HAMBURG // LONDON // LOS ANGELES // TOKYO

Loveless Volume 5

Created by Yun Kouga

Translation - Ray Yoshimoto
English Adaptation - Christine Boylan
Retouch and Lettering - Star Print Brokers
Production Artist - Michael Paolilli
Graphic Designer - Monalisa De Asis

Editor - Lillian Diaz-Przybyl
Digital Imaging Manager - Chris Buford
Pre-Production Supervisor - Erika Terriquez
Art Director - Anne Marie Horne
Production Manager - Elisabeth Brizzi
Managing Editor - Vy Nguyen
VP of Production - Ron Klamert
Editor-in-Chief - Rob Tokar
Publisher - Mike Kiley
President and C.O.O. - John Parker
C.E.O. and Chief Creative Officer - Stuart Levy

A  Manga

TOKYOPOP Inc.
5900 Wilshire Blvd. Suite 2000
Los Angeles, CA 90036

E-mail: info@TOKYOPOP.com
Come visit us online at www.TOKYOPOP.com

ISBN: 978-1-59816-225-7

First TOKYOPOP printing: May 2007

10 9 8 7 6 5 4 3 2

Printed in the USA

......
MUNCH
MUNCH
MOM.
I'M GOING.

The Sacrifice Chapters
Chapter 1

I'M SORRY, MOM.

I...

...I NEED TO KNOW THE TRUTH.

HUH?

WHERE'S RITSUKA-KUN?

NO ONE CALLED THE OFFICE TO REPORT HIM ABSENT...

HERE.

THANK YOU, MISTER.

UH-HUH.

BEING IN THE PARK MAKES ME CONSPICUOUS.

I stick out too much.

AND I CAN'T SLEEP OUTSIDE LIKE A BUM.

WHERE CAN I...

... SLEEP.

WHERE CAN I SLEEP...

PLEASE LEAVE A MESSAGE AFTER THE TONE.
...BUT IT'S JUST AN ANSWERING MACHINE.

MAYBE HERE...
I can sleep!
...I CAN BLEND IN. HIDE.
Z Z Z Z

Riiiiiiiiing
ZZZZZZ...
Stare
NEXT TRAIN ARRIVING ON PLATFORM 4.
PLEASE STAY BEHIND THE WHITE LINE.
Riiiiing
ZZZZZ...
YOUNG MAN.
THE TRAIN'S HERE. WAKE UP!
Riiiiing
Ack!
Yeek!

YOU'RE GETTING ON, RIGHT?
UH...
WHERE ARE YOU GOING? GRANNY WILL RIDE WITH YOU.
THAT'S OKAY.
IT'S NO GOOD IF YOU SLEEP THROUGH YOUR STOP, RIGHT?
I-I'M FINE.

WELL...
THIS IS MY STOP.

OOH HOO!

TAKE CARE.
DON'T OVERSLEEP.

WHAT...
...AM I DOING?

I NEED TO FIND...
...A PLACE TO SLEEP.

IT STINGS...
YOU BURNED YOURSELF AGAIN, KIO?
I LIKE HOW HOT WATER MAKES THE PAINT MELT EVENLY.
I USE LUKEWARM WATER.
AND THAT'S WHY YOUR TEXTURE IS SO IRREGULAR, SOU-CHAN! HAPHAZARD!
HAPHAZARD.
I LIKE THAT.
HMMM.
I HAVE TO ADMIT...
...YOU DID BRING OUT A NICE... FLAVOR.

I LIKE THIS PINKISH COLOR.
WHAT IS IT?
ONE OF THE COPPERS.
REALLY. WHAT'S IT CALLED?

MEAT.
IT REMINDS ME OF BACON.
PIG MEAT?
NO, THE ARTIST BACON.
OHHH.
YOU'RE DOING THIS ON PURPOSE.
11:05
11:15
出口
カタタン
NOD
タン…
NOD, nod
タタン…
Z z z

Ngh...

THIS IS NO GOOD.

I NEED A PLACE TO SLEEP...!!

I DIDN'T WANT TO RESORT TO THIS, BUT...

Grit

...IT CAN'T BE HELPED.

I CAN HEAR THE RAIN.
AGHH...
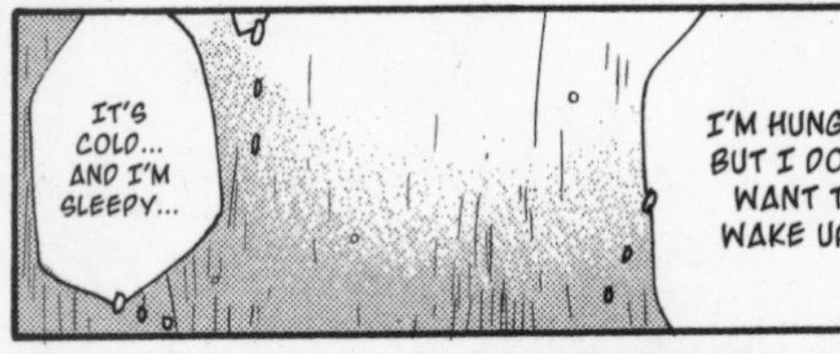
I'M HUNGRY. BUT I DON'T WANT TO WAKE UP...
IT'S COLD... AND I'M SLEEPY...

モゾ
I DON'T WANT TO LEAVE MY NEST...
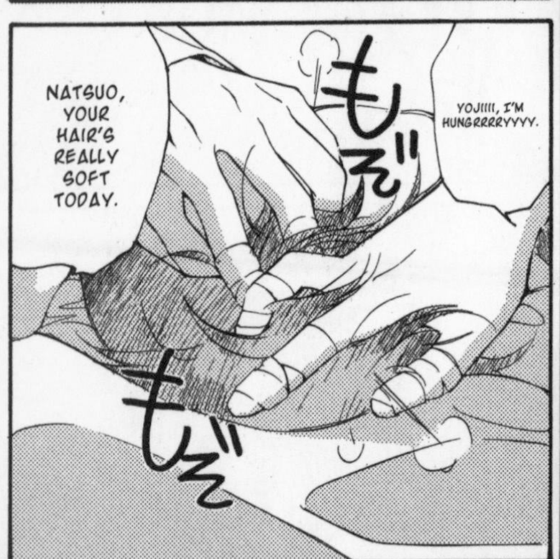
YOJIIII, I'M HUNGRRRRYYYY.
もぞ
NATSUO, YOUR HAIR'S REALLY SOFT TODAY.
もぞ

HUH?!

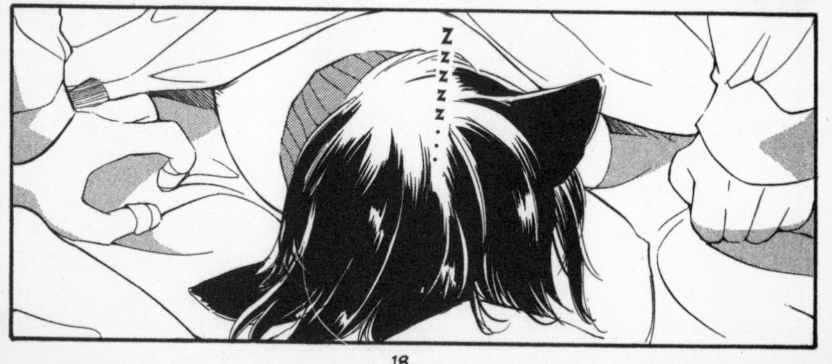

WHAT'S RITSUKA DOING HERE?
SHHH.
I DON'T KNOW! HOW'D HE SNEAK IN?
ZZZZZ...
......
HIS HAIR IS SOFT...
EVEN THOUGH IT'S BLACK.
WHAT DOES THE COLOR MATTER?
BLACK HAIR JUST SEEMS SO... COARSE.
ギャアアア

WHERE...
...AM...
...I?
HEEEEY.
SOME-BODY...
...IS ANYBODY THERE...?
!...
Clonk
OW.
THERE'S SOME-THING...
Clonk
AGH!
HERE, TOO.
OW!
IT'S A DEAD END.

SEIMEI!!
RITSUKA.
OVER HERE... RI-TSUKA.
THIS WAY.
SEIMEI!
I'VE FINALLY FOUND YOU!!
I'VE BEEN LOOKING FOR YOU ALL THIS TIME.
COME HERE, RITSUKA.
EIMEI!!
WAIT!! IT'S REALLY DARK OVER THERE.
SEIMEI, WHAT'S THERE...

...HUH?
HOW DID I GET ALL WET?
IT'S KINDA... HOT...
SEIMEI!!
Ooh, 19 chain reactions!

ガタ

RITSUKA?
ガア...
......
I HAD A BAD DREAM...

ARE YOU ALL RIGHT?
NNN...
AND WHAT ARE YOU DOING HERE?

THE DOOR WAS OPEN...
THAT'S NOT WHAT I'M TALKING ABOUT! WHY ARE YOU SLEEPING HERE?

YEAH.

TONIGHT I'M GOING TO PLAY WISDOM RESURRECTION.

I'M GOING TO GET CLOSE TO SEPTIMAL MOON.

I'M NOT GOING HOME TONIGHT.

WHAT ABOUT YOUR PARENTS?

MY MOTHER'S A SHUT-IN.

SHE HARDLY LEAVES HER ROOM, LET ALONE THE HOUSE. SHE WON'T EVEN NOTICE...

...THAT I'M GONE.

I WONDER ... IF RIT-CHAN ...

...IS COMING TONIGHT?

Tra La La

OH, NAGISA-TAN.

GOOD EVENING, SEVEN-TAN.

WHY NOT? I SAW HIS PICTURE.
HE'S MY TYPE, AND IT'S A RARE ONE--BOTH CUTE AND GLOOMY. ❤
HE SHOULD HURRY UP AND DITCH SOUBI.
IT'D BE MORE FUN IF HE USED THE PROPER LOVELESS FIGHTER.

....
Hmph!

YOU ABSOLUTELY WON'T SAY...
Ha Ha
...THAT YOU HATE RITSU.

"It's Ritsu. Can I come by tonight?"
Whaaaaaaaat?

One new message.
I WONDER WHO IT IS?
tweedledeedaling
OH.

One new message.
dingalingaling
OH.
AGAIN...

Message erased.
POOF
I WISH OTHER PEOPLE WOULDN'T STIR THINGS UP SO.
IT'S MY JOB TO MAKE FIRST CONTACT WITH RITSUKA.
But I told him to come.
YOU'RE SUCH A SCROOGE, SEVEN-TAN.

"Loveless is online."

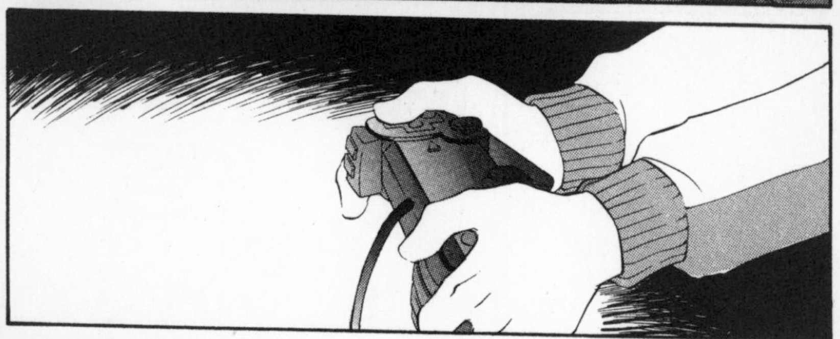

The Sacrifice Chapters
Chapter 2

YOU'RE PLAYING AS A THIEF? AMATEUR.
I KNOW WHAT I'M DOING.
WHAT WEAPONS DO YOU HAVE?
SHUT UP.
I'M SERIOUS!!
LET ME PLAY.
JUST FOR A MINUTE.
LET ME SEE YOUR STATUS.
YOUR INTERRUPTIONS ARE IRRITATING RITSUKA.
THAT'S RIGHT!

STAY OUT OF MY WAY!
......
SCARY.
heh!
WELCOME, LOVELESS.

MY NAME IS RITSUKA.
!!
7 LV.00000
RITSU LV.1000
0000
IT'S NAGISA-SENSEI!

AOYAGI RITSUKA.
WHAT?
LET ME SEE.
EVEN HER SCREEN NAME'S NAGISA. IT'S DEFINITELY HER!
SOUBI, TYPE FOR ME.
Yes sir.
NA...
NAGISA-SENSEI...
KNOCK IT OFF.
SHE DOESN'T MISS YOU. SHE DOESN'T CARE ABOUT YOU.
......!!
WHAT--
WHAT THE HELL DO YOU KNOW ABOUT IT, SOUBI?!

I DON'T KNOW!!
HAS SHE BOTHERED TO CALL YOU?
...NO. YOU'RE RIGHT. I KNOW.
NAGISA... SENSEI!?
TODAY... YOU'RE GOING TO TELL ME EVERYTHING.
ABOUT THE ONE WHO KILLED SEIMEI. EVERY-THING.
I'M JUST HERE TO OBSERVE. DON'T MIND ME.
I'M HERE TO OBSERVE, TOO!!
...WHY ARE THERE THREE OF YOU HERE...
So tall...
THINK OF THEM AS TWO OLD, STONE IDOLS. GARGOYLES, EVEN.

I FIGURED IT OUT... SEIMEI WAS IN SEPTIMAL MOON, WASN'T HE?
HOW COULD YOU JUST STAND THERE AFTER KILLING ONE OF YOUR OWN?
DON'T GET MAD AT ME. I'M NOT A MEMBER.
NEITHER AM I.
YOU ARE CORRECT. SEIMEI WAS A MEMBER.
...NGH.
ガタ
SOUBI?
I'LL TYPE.
NATSUO!
YOUR ARM STILL HURTS. I CAN DO IT FOR YOU.

SO... SEIMEI REALLY WAS A MEMBER.
TYPE, "DO YOU KNOW WHO THE KILLER IS?"
......
HE KNOWS WHAT TO TYPE.
Bah!
DO YOU KNOW WHO THE KILLER IS?
I DON'T KNOW. BUT THERE'S SOMEONE WHO MAY...
... NUMBER FOUR.
THE PERSON CLOSEST TO SEIMEI.
I MIGHT LET YOU TWO MEET, IF YOU AGREE TO MY DEMANDS.
WHAT DEMANDS?
YOU TELL ME EVERYTHING YOU KNOW ABOUT SEIMEI.
IS THIS A TRICK? YOU ALREADY KNOW ALL ABOUT SEIMEI.

WELL, I WONDER ABOUT THAT.
OUR JOB IS TO GATHER AND ORGANIZE INFORMATION.
I WANT TO KNOW EVERYTHING ABOUT WHAT YOU AND SEIMEI DID.
WHAT SEIMEI AND I...
...DID?
CAN YOU REALLY TALK ABOUT IT?
SEIMEI IS DEAD. HE IS LOST FOREVER.
DO YOU HAVE THE COURAGE TO RESURRECT SEIMEI IN YOUR WORDS, EVEN THOUGH YOU CAN NEVER REVIVE HIM IN THE FLESH?
...WAHH...
THIS RITSU-SENSEI...

I SEE HE'S IN GOOD FORM.
HE HAS A PARTICULARLY NASTY WAY OF SAYING THINGS.
DON'T MIND HIM, RITSUKA.
THE ONLY THING HE LOVES IS HURTING PEOPLE.
WELL, I'M NOT GOING TO GET HURT.
I WILL NOT GET HURT.
MY ONLY GOAL IS TO FIND THE KILLER.

FIRST I'M GOING TO FIND THE GUY WHO KILLED SEIMEI. THEN I'M GOING TO GET REVENGE.

IT'S NOT SOME NOBLE JUSTICE. IT'S A GRUDGE.

ANGER AT BEING LEFT SO ALONE.

IS IT RECORDING?
Oopsy daisy!
YES. YES IT IS... OKAY.

NOW THEN.
LET'S HAVE HIM TELL US ABOUT SEIMEI.

HOW MUCH DID WE KNOW ABOUT SEIMEI?
PERHAPS NOTHING.
THERE'S A SIDE OF SEIMEI THAT ONLY RITSUKA KNEW.

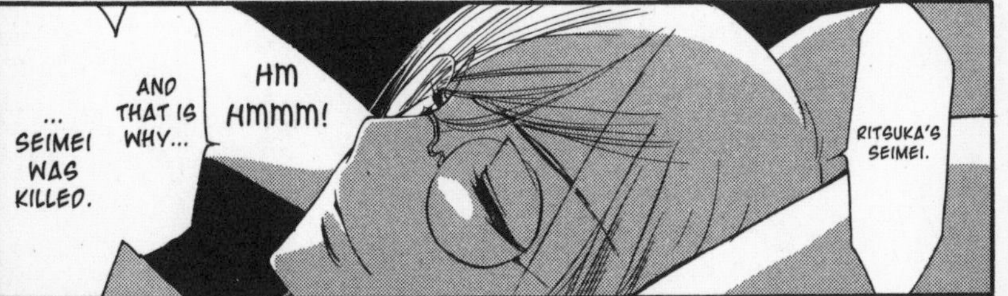
RITSUKA'S SEIMEI.
HM HMMM!
AND THAT IS WHY...
...SEIMEI WAS KILLED.

......

......

THIS SEIMEI...

WHAT KIND OF PERSON WAS HE?

SEIMEI WAS MY GOD.

...I HARDLY EVER SAW HIM ASLEEP.
HE ALWAYS WOKE UP BEFORE ME, AND WENT TO BED AFTER ME.
GOOD MORNING, RITSUKA.
IF YOU DON'T WAKE UP NOW, YOU'LL BE LATE.
SEIMEI DID EVERYTHING THAT MY MOTHER DIDN'T DO.
ANYTHING THAT I DIDN'T KNOW, SEIMEI WOULD TEACH ME.
jiiiii
jijijiiii
RITSUKA, DO YOU KNOW WHAT THIS SOUND IS?
jiiiiii
NO... WHAT IS IT?
SEIMEI'S HANDS WERE LARGE AND WARM. IT WAS A LITTLE EMBARRASSING FOR ME, BUT...
...HE LIKED TO HOLD MY HAND WHEN WE WALKED.
Jiiii
IT'S THE CRY OF THE MOLE CRICKET.
Jiiii
MOLE CRICKET?
Jiiii
YOU AREN'T GOING TO COME IN, SEIMEI?
I DON'T THINK I'D FIT...
HE ALWAYS PLAYED WITH ME.
WHAT IS THIS?
LOOK, IT'S WEIRD.
THIS WEBSITE IS REALLY FUN.
WE HAD SEPARATE ROOMS, BUT WE WERE ALWAYS TOGETHER.

NOD
YOU'RE NOT GOING TO SLEEP YET, SEIMEI?
nod
NOT YET... I'M DOING SOMETHING NOW...
I ALWAYS SLEPT IN SEIMEI'S BED.
I CAN'T STAY... AWAKE...
G'NIGHT...
Zzzzz
HMM. 'NIGHT.
MY MOTHER WAS MUCH... BETTER... WHEN SEIMEI WAS AROUND. AND WHEN SHE WAS BAD, HE WOULD PROTECT ME.
HE'D GO WITH ME TO THE HOSPITAL, TOO.
I WAS MUCH BETTER WHEN SEIMEI WAS AROUND.

FINISHED.
IS THE BANDAGE TOO TIGHT?
IT'S FINE.
RITSUKA.
YES?
I'M SORRY I CAME HOME LATE TODAY.
IT'S OKAY.
IF MOTHER ACTS UP WHEN I'M NOT HERE, YOU GO OUTSIDE.
OKAY...
I'LL DO THAT FROM NOW ON...

HOW ARE YOU GOING TO TAKE A BATH WITH THAT WRIST WRAPPED UP?
I CAN DO IT.
IT'S OKAY.
DID YOU EAT?
I HAD MCDONALD'S.
SHALL I MAKE YOU SOMETHING?
I'M OKAY. I'M FULL.
THEN... WHAT SHALL WE DO?
MAYBE I SHOULD SERVICE YOU, HUH?
SEIMEI!
IT TICKLES!
MAYBE WE'LL GO TO SLEEP NOW.
NUH-UHH.
I'M GOING TO TAKE A BATH.
THEN I'LL GIVE YOU A MASSAGE FIRST.
squeeze
SEIMEI!
THAT TICKLES!

RITSUKA.
YOU HAVEN'T DONE ANYTHING WRONG.
POOR THING. YOU SHOULD KNOW THAT.
IT WAS FUN WHEN SEIMEI WAS AROUND.
I WAS NEVER LONELY.
I DIDN'T HATE ANYONE BACK THEN.

HE WAS EXTREMELY OBSESSIVE-COMPULSIVE.

HE COULDN'T EVEN TOUCH ANYONE ELSE, MUCH LESS SLEEP IN THE SAME BED AS SOMEONE.

SO? WHICH ONE?

WHICH ONE WAS THE REAL SEIMEI?

He's neither real nor fake. Seimei is just Seimei.
SEIMEI HAD A SIDE THAT I HAD NEVER SEEN.
I NEVER KNEW.
BUT THAT DOESN'T MATTER. THAT DOESN'T HURT ME.
He was the only one. There was only one Seimei.

The Sacrifice Chapters
Chapter 3

WHAT KIND OF GUY WAS SEIMEI?
ARE YOU REALLY INTERESTED?
A LITTLE.

THEN I'M NOT TELLING.
WHAT THE FUCK?
YOU'VE GOT A REAL ATTITUDE PROBLEM!
YOU COULD SIT OUTSIDE HIS DOOR A THOUSAND YEARS, AND SEIMEI STILL WOULDN'T TALK TO YOU.
WHAT DO YOU MEAN BY THAT?!
AHH.
SO THAT'S HOW IT WAS.
HMPH. BUT HE'S DEAD NOW.
HE HAS NO MORE POWER.
END OF STORY.
I WONDER...

HMPH.
WHAT ARE YOU DOING?
YOJI...?
Huh huh huh...
I'M JUST STICKING WITH YOU, KID.
YOU DUMMY!
ALL WE DID WAS TOUCH OUR LIPS TOGETHER IN FRIENDSHIP.
SMOOCH!
!!

WAH!
Hmph!
SEIMEI CAN'T DO A THING.
YOU DON'T UNDER-STAND.
THIS IS SEIMEI'S ARM.
WHA!
THESE ARE SEIMEI'S LEGS.
!!
EVEN IF SEIMEI ISN'T HERE, HIS ORDERS ARE CARRIED OUT.
LET GO OF ME!

...THAT'S WHAT IT MEANS TO BE DOMINATED.
smile ♥
バタン
SLAM
WHY YOU...
LET ME IN!
bam
bam
bam
LET HIM IN, SOUBI.
NO ONE WHO HARMS RITSUKA MAY ENTER.
スタスタ
OH. I SEE.
THEN I'LL LEAVE, TOO.
THIS IS YOUR ROOM AFTER ALL.
BUH-BYE!
WAH!
DON'T BE MEAN TO EACH OTHER!

I--

I CAN HANDLE A KISS!

EVERY TIME YOU DO IT TO ME, SOUBI, YOU SAY IT BRINGS US CLOSER.

EVERY TIME? SOUNDS LIKE MANY TIMES.
YUP.
Yikes...
TO BECOME CLOSER?
THAT'S RIGHT, TO BECOME CLOSER.
Waah!
YOU'RE FAST, HUH?
A BIT.

YOU CAN ALL WATCH, BUT KEEP IT QUIET.
BECAUSE THE NEXT PERSON WHO INTERRUPTS IS GETTING THROWN OUT FOR REAL. I DON'T CARE WHO IT IS!!

IT WASN'T JUST A KISS. I MEAN, I THOUGHT YOJI WAS GOING TO STRIP HIM...
YES, SIR.
YES, SIR.

RITSUKA'S GOING TO NEED SPECIAL HANDLING.
OVER-ATTACHMENT... IT GOES WAY BEYOND BROTHERLY LOVE.
WHAT?! IT'S ONLY NATURAL FOR THE OLDER BROTHER TO PROTECT THE YOUNGER.
HEY! I DON'T LIKE SECRETS.

WHEN SEIMEI WAS FIVE...

...HIS YOUNGER BROTHER RITSUKA WAS BORN.

HOW DID SEIMEI FEEL ABOUT RITSUKA THEN?

SO NOW YOU HAVE SOUBI-KUN WITH YOU.

ARE YOU SURE YOU CAN KEEP HIM SATISFIED?

HIS VOICE IS SORE FROM SCREAMING WITH PLEASURE EVERY DAY.

BUT THANKS FOR YOUR CONCERN.

NATSUO! DON'T TYPE THAT!
THAT'S NOT WHAT I SAID.
Screaming with pleasure?!
BUT SOUBI SAID...
THAT'S RIGHT. I DID.
...to type it.
YOU'VE MESSED UP MY PERSONA.
LOVELESS...
I HAVE A GREAT DEAL OF INFORMATION FOR YOU.
BUT FIRST THERE ARE SOME THINGS I WANT TO ASK YOU DIRECTLY.
DO YOU LOVE SEIMEI?
WOULD YOU STILL LOVE HIM IF HE BETRAYED YOU?

I LOVE HIM!!
I DON'T THINK SEIMEI WOULD EVER BETRAY ME.
BUT IF THAT ANSWER DOESN'T SATISFY YOU...
...HE COULD BETRAY ME...
HURT ME, KILL ME.
BUT I WOULD STILL LOVE SEIMEI.
OH, RITSUKA. YOU REALLY DON'T KNOW...
...DO YOU?
WE HOPED THAT IF WE PROVOKED YOU, SEIMEI WOULD SHOW UP.

WE SUSPECT THAT SEIMEI...

...NH...

...IS STILL ALIVE.

Seimei...

...is alive?!

THEY USED DENTAL RECORDS TO IDENTIFY THE BODY.
IT WAS BURNT TOO BADLY TO DO A CONCLUSIVE DNA TEST.
...BUT THE POLICE... SAID...
...THAT WAS HIS BODY...
WE BELIEVE NO SATISFACTORY IDENTIFICATION WAS MADE.
AND WE DON'T BELIEVE THAT SEIMEI WOULD HAVE DIED THAT EASILY.
BUT... YOU JUST SAID...
...SEPTIMAL MOON KILLED HIM!!
WE HAD DECIDED ON A DEATH SENTENCE. IT WAS A UNANIMOUS VOTE.
BUT BEFORE WE COULD EXECUTE HIM, SEIMEI DIED.

UNAN-
IMOUS
VOTE?
WHY?
WHY...
WHY
WOULD
YOU KILL
SEIMEI?!
ONE DAY,
SOMEONE
SHOULD
TELL YOU
OF HIS
SINS.
WHAT
SINS...?
SEIMEI
WOULDN'T
DO ANYTHING
TO WARRANT
A DEATH
PENALTY!!
IF
THAT'S
WHAT YOU
THINK,
THEN WHY
DON'T
YOU ASK
SOUBI?
SOUBI
KNOWS
EVERYTHING.

SEIMEI IS ALIVE?!
I CAN SEE HIM AGAIN?
AGAIN?
IF HE'S ALIVE, WHY HASN'T HE COME HOME?
WHY DOES HE LEAVE ME BY MYSELF?
DOES HE HATE ME?
NO. THERE'S NO WAY HE'S ALIVE.
HE DIED.
IF HE WERE ALIVE HE'D BE HERE.
MY MISSION IS TO CONFIRM THAT SEIMEI FAKED HIS OWN DEATH.
FOUR'S MISSION IS TO CONFIRM SEIMEI'S ACTUAL DEATH.
THAT INCLUDES ARRESTING SEIMEI'S MURDERER.
IF SEIMEI IS STILL ALIVE, WE'LL HAVE TO KILL HIM.
NUMBER FOUR WILL ALSO EXECUTE THAT SENTENCE.

SEIMEI WAS SUPPOSED TO HAVE DIED.
BUT WHAT IF HE DIDN'T?
WHAT IF HE'S SOMEWHERE, SUFFERING, EVEN MORE ALONE THAN I AM?
tremble
THEY ARE... MONSTROUS.
JUST WHEN RITSUKA HAD FINALLY ACCEPTED SEIMEI'S DEATH...
ARE YOU ALL RIGHT?
STILL ALIVE AND ABOUT TO DIE? OR ALREADY DEAD?
I'M NOT SURE WHICH ONE'S WORSE...

The Sacrifice Chapters
Chapter 4

Riiiiing

Riiiiiiing

Riiiiiiing

Riiiiiiing
Riiiiiiing
SHUT UP...

ギイ…
Riiiiiiiing

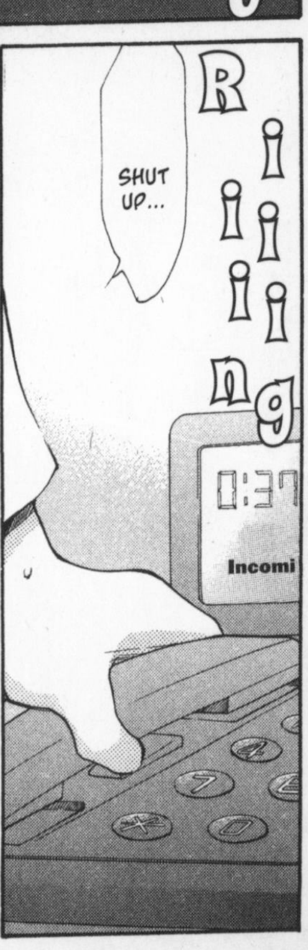
Riiiiiing
SHUT UP...
0:37
Incomi

......
...HELLO?
WHO IS THIS...?

WHERE IS RITSUKA?

WHERE'S RITSUKA?
Click

......
......
RITSUKA?

Ritsuka?

SOUBI!
YES.
JUST ASK HIM. HE KNOWS EVERYTHING.
BUT SOUBI WON'T TELL THE TRUTH.
YOU'RE RIGHT.
IF YOU KNOW SOMETHING, THEN TELL ME.
IS SEIMEI... IS HE REALLY... STILL ALIVE?!

THIS IS A WASTE OF TIME.
YOU'RE GETTING SO OVERWROUGHT, BUT THERE'S NO PROOF.
AND YOU CAN'T BELIEVE SOUBI ANYWAY.
EVERY-THING HE SAYS IS A LIE OR A JOKE.
SOUBI!!
ANSWER ME!
Won't work.
Won't work.
It won't work.
SEE?
THEY'RE SAYING SO, TOO.
AH...

YOU GUYS HAVE NOTHING TO DO WITH THIS.
Hey, he shut it off!
Awww...
I BELIEVE YOU.
SOUBI, I'LL BELIEVE YOU.
SO, PLEASE ...
...DON'T BETRAY ME.
ANSWER ME.
IS SEIMEI ...
...STILL ALIVE...?

HE'S DEAD.
SEIMEI DIED.
THIS IS THE TRUTH.
......
......

Twitch
Riiiing
... IS THAT...
...MY PHONE?!
WHO COULD IT BE AT THIS HOUR...
Yuiko
IT'S YUIKO!
HELLO? YUIKO?!
RITSUKA-KUN? WHERE ARE YOU?!
WHAT IS IT? WHAT HAPPENED?
YOUR MOTHER...
YOUR MOTHER IS LOOKING FOR YOU, RITSUKA-KUN.
SHE LOOKED UP THE CLASS DIRECTORY AND HAS BEEN CALLING EVERYONE.

THANKS, YUIKO.

SORRY YOU WERE WOKEN UP.

HOW DID SHE...

THAT'S OKAY, RITSUKA-KUN.

MY MOTHER FOUND OUT.

SHE'S CALLING EVERYONE IN MY CLASS.

WHOA, IT'S ONE A.M.!

WHY WOULD SHE CALL THE WHOLE CLASS, INSTEAD OF JUST YOUR FRIENDS?

I DON'T HAVE ANY FRIENDS.

What a weirdo.

HA

WHY, OF ALL DAYS? WHY TODAY?

THERE'S NO WAY SHE WOULD COME INTO MY ROOM THIS LATE AT NIGHT!!

SHE'LL CASTIGATE YOU.

CASTIGATE?

I'LL WALK YOU HOME, RITSUKA.

WHAT'S THAT?

IT'S OKAY!!

YOU'RE GOING HOME, RIGHT?

I AM! MY MOTHER IS WORRIED.

I'LL WALK YOU HOME.

I CAN GO HOME BY MYSELF. STAY HERE!

STOP IGNORING US!!
Booo
booo
Booo
WHERE DO YOU THINK RITSUKA GOT THOSE INJURIES?

WHERE ARE YOU GOING?
I'M GOING TO WALK RITSUKA HOME. FROM A DISTANCE.
Pfft!
SO YOU'RE GOING TO TAIL HIM!

IT'S HIS MOTHER.

IT'S TIME FOR LITTLE KIDS TO BE IN BED.
GO TO SLEEP.

HE'S AN ABUSED KID!!
kyaaa
Kya kyaa
HE'S A MORON FOR KEEPING QUIET ABOUT IT. WHY NOT KICK HER ASS?
OF COURSE!

The Sacrifice Chapters
Chapter 5

WHAT AN IDIOT. HE SHOULD JUST KILL HIS MOM.
...LETTING HER HURT HIM LIKE THAT.
Giggle
TOTALLY.
THERE'S NO WAY HE'D BEAT HER IN A FISTFIGHT, THOUGH.
RITSUKA'S SUCH AN IDIOT.

BIG M
ルテール
2F

MIMURO, WHERE DO YOU PUT ALL THAT?
くしゃ*
HM?

HOW CAN YOU EAT SO MUCH AT THIS HOUR?
WHERE DOES IT ALL GO?

I'M TIRED.
SO IF I DON'T EAT, I'LL JUST FALL ASLEEP.

DO YOU WANT TO GO HOME AND SLEEP?
WHY DON'T YOU DO THAT, IF YOU'RE TIRED?
Yawwwn
IF I CAN JUST LEAVE, WHY ARE WE HERE IN THE FIRST PLACE?
WHY DON'T WE JUST GO HOME BEFORE HE GETS HERE, THEN?
WE CAN JUST GO HOME AND SLEEP INSTEAD OF WAITING.
AND LEAVE NISEI HERE?
ズー
WE CAN'T DO THAT.
SORRY TO KEEP YOU WAITING.
WERE YOU ABLE TO MAKE THE CALL?
YES, NO PROBLEM.
Smile
EVERYTHING'S GOING AS PLANNED.

MURO-SENPAI.

WILL YOU DO THIS JOB FOR ME?

THAT'S WHY I'VE BEEN WAITING HERE.

...SO... WE'RE GOING, THEN.

YES, MEI-SAN.

DON'T LEAVE ANYTHING BEHIND.

THAT'S THE END OF TODAY'S LESSON.

PLEASE REVIEW IT THOROUGHLY, ALL RIGHT, MEI-SAN?

......

ガタ

ガタ

OF COURSE, IF YOU GO INTO BATTLE AFTER THIS, THAT'S A LESSON AS WELL.

IF THE SITUATION BECOMES DANGEROUS, PLEASE DON'T HESITATE TO ESCAPE IMMEDIATELY.

IF WE FEEL WE CAN WIN, THOUGH, SHALL WE CONTINUE ON?

THAT'S UNLIKELY.
THE ONLY THING MORE DANGEROUS THAN THE MISSION ITSELF IS HOPE OF ITS SUCCESS.
WE WON'T KNOW IF WE DON'T TRY.
SOME OUTCOMES WE KNOW IN ADVANCE OF THE ATTEMPT.
YOUR OPPONENT IS LOVELESS. AGATSUMA SOUBI. HE CANNOT BE DEFEATED... BY THE USUAL MEANS.
......
UNFORTUNATELY, AT MEI-SAN'S LEVEL, THE BEST WE CAN HOPE IS TO DELAY HIM, OR GAIN SOME NEW INFORMATION ABOUT HIS POWER.
SO HE'S POWER-FUL?

YOU'D HAVE TO BE AT MY LEVEL OF STRENGTH-- AT LEAST-- IN ORDER TO BATTLE HIM.
THIS IS A READING LIST.
Heh!
HAVE IT COMPLETED BY OUR NEXT MEETING. YOUR VOCABULARY ISN'T WHAT IT OUGHT TO BE, MEI-SAN.
......
I HATE HIM...
WHY DO YOU DO WHAT THAT CREEP SAYS? DO YOU LIKE HIM, MIMURO?
HE IS A FELLOW STUDENT.
MIMURO?
......

I'M A COMPLICATED PERSON. YOU EXPECT EVERYONE TO BE AS SIMPLE AS YOU ARE.

I THINK NISEI'S ATTRACTIVE, EVEN THOUGH WE'RE BOTH BOYS. AND THERE ARE OTHER FEELINGS THAT I HAVEN'T YET SORTED THROUGH.

IT DOESN'T COME DOWN TO JUST LIKING OR HATING.

I LET YOU CALL ME BY NAME. ISN'T THAT GOOD ENOUGH?
MEI.
YOU HAPPY NOW? MEEEEI.
......
hmmm...
......
IT'S KIND OF CREEPY TO USE OUR REAL NAMES.
......
...ALL RIGHT, THEN.
THAT'S GOOD.
THAT...
THAT'S GOOD.

IT FEELS EXTREMELY... UNSTEADY, I WOULD SAY... OR RATHER, THERE'S SOMETHING UNCERTAIN ABOUT IT.

ARE YOU GOING TO BE OKAY IN BATTLE? IF I JOIN UP WITH YOU, AM I GOING TO MAKE IT HOME IN ONE PIECE?

NO MATTER WHO WE FACE?

DON'T WORRY... I'LL TRY HARD.

HE TREATS ME LIKE A BABY, BUT I'M--

huff

ギギーッ

IT'S NO USE APOLOGIZING... YOU'RE STILL PUNISHED.

...HERE IT COMES...

YOU'RE TRYING TO FOOL ME AGAIN.

WHERE WERE YOU?!

IF YOU HATE BEING IN THIS HOUSE SO MUCH, THEN GET OUT AND STAY OUT!

I CAN'T CONTROL MYSELF.

I'M SO ANGRY, I...

I CAN'T DO THIS. PLEASE, STOP!

tremble

tremble

I'M NOT GOING.

WHAT DID YOU DO, RUN AWAY AND THEN CHICKEN OUT?!

GET OUT OF MY HOUSE!

I'M SORRY.

tremble

...BUT I'M NOT GOING ANYWHERE..
...THIS IS MY HOME...
STOP IT. STOP IT. I HAVE TO STOP.
I CAN'T HIT THIS CHILD.
I GAVE BIRTH TO THIS BOY, I CAN'T...
GET OUT! GET OUT!!
A CHILD SHOULD LISTEN TO HIS MOTHER, RIGHT?!
THAT'S RIGHT!!
A CHILD MUST LISTEN TO HIS MOTHER.
OR HE'LL NEVER LEARN ANYTHING! HE'LL GROW UP WILD! YOU KNOW THAT ALL TOO WELL.
I WAS RAISED IN A MUCH STRICTER ENVIRONMENT!

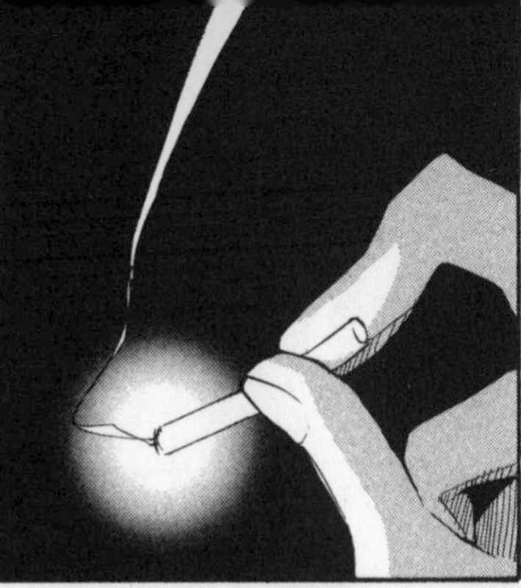

...THAT'S WHAT I HEAR.
SO WHAT'S YOUR STORY, MISAKI-SAN?

crash
Thud

WHY CAN'T YOU LISTEN TO WHAT I SAY!!

WHAT ARE YOU LOOKING AT?! IF YOU HAVE SOMETHING TO SAY, THEN SAY IT!!

....
AN ABUSIVE PARENT...
...WAS PROBABLY AN ABUSED CHILD.

MOTHER, STOP IT!
THEN GET OUT!!
NO!
GET OUT!
NO!
I DON'T WANT TO.
I'M NOT LEAVING!
THEN DIE!
NO!
DIE! DIE! JUST DIE!!
Cough
I'M NOT DYING!!
Cough
WHY WON'T YOU LISTEN TO ME!
I SAID DIE!
......
Cough
Cough
DIE!!

IF I KNEW YOU'D TURN OUT LIKE THIS I NEVER WOULD'VE HAD YOU!

......

SHE COULDN'T POSSIBLY HAVE THE STRENGTH TO KEEP THIS UP...

WHEN SHE GETS TIRED, SHE'LL STOP...

YOU'RE MY MISTAKE!

I SHOULD'VE CUT YOU OUT!

I DON'T NEED TO LISTEN TO THIS. THAT'S NOT MY MOTHER TALKING.

cough

DOES AOYAGI-SAN REALIZE WHAT TIME IT IS?
IT'S A NUISANCE TO THE NEIGHBORHOOD. THAT BOY MUST STILL BE IN GRADE SCHOOL.
MAYBE WE SHOULD CALL THE POLICE?
NO. THERE'S NOTHING WE CAN DO...
HE'S HER CHILD. WE CAN'T INTERFERE.
CHILD ABUSE. ❤
I LOOKED IT UP ON THE INTERNET. ❤
AAHHH.
INSTEAD OF TAKING CARE OF THEIR KIDS, THEY BEAT THEM UP. BASICALLY.
HE SHOULD JUST FIGHT BACK.
WE WOULD!! BUT A KID CAN'T HIT HIS MOM, I GUESS.

READ THIS. MOTHERS EXPERIENCE ACUTE STRESS.

ooh hooo!

SUCK IT UP! IT'S NOT LIKE THEY DON'T KNOW WHAT THEY'RE GETTING INTO. BE RESPONSIBLE!

IF SHE DIDN'T WANT HIM, SHE SHOULDN'T HAVE HAD HIM. ADULTS ARE SO THOUGHT-LESS.

AREN'T THEY.

They put themselves first, always.

IT'S PROBABLY MORE HUMANE TO ABANDON HIM THAN TO BEAT HIM. WHAT AN IDIOT.

Y'KNOW?

BUT IF YOU WERE ALONE...
...IT MIGHT BE IMPOSSIBLE.
DON'T COME IN...
...GO AWAY.

The Sacrifice Chapters
Chapter 6

IT GOT QUIET...

DON'T COME IN!
DON'T COME IN!!
I DON'T WANT TO BE NEAR YOU!!
MOTHER...
I'M NOT CRAZY.
I MEAN WHAT I SAY!

M-MOTHER... IF YOU DON'T...
...DRY OFF... YOU'LL CATCH COLD.
LEAVE ME ALONE!
I--HOW CAN I DO THIS TO HIM? THIS IS WRONG!!

MY ARMS HURT. MY HANDS HURT. THEY BURN. FROM BEATING MY SON.
BUT I CAN'T STOP MYSELF!!

MOTHER, PLEASE COME OUT.
I'M TIRED...

SO...
WRONG, RITSUKA.
WHEN SOMEONE CAN'T CONTROL HIS VIOLENT ACTIONS...
WHA...
SHH...!!
...YOU SHOULD FLEE FROM HIM.

Doki
WHA ...
Doki doki
IF YOU GO NEAR HER, THINGS WILL JUST ESCALATE.
IF YOUR MOTHER'S TELLING YOU TO GET AWAY, AND YOU STILL STAND OUTSIDE HER DOOR...

...IT'S SUICIDE, RITSUKA.
WHAT... WHAT ARE YOU SAYING?
YOU'RE THE ONE BEING SUICIDAL.
Unlawful entry!!

WHAT ARE YOU GOING TO DO IF MOTHER CATCHES YOU OUT HERE?

NOTHING.
I WON'T DO ANYTHING.

THERE'S NO REASONING WITH HYSTERICS. YOU SHOULD JUST LEAVE HER BE.
I CAN'T.
I CAN'T LEAVE HER....

SHE'LL BE SO...
...LONELY.

プルルルル
Riiiiiiiiiiiiiiing
ルルル!
1:27
Incoming Call
ル
ビク
プルルル
Riiiiiiing
Riiiiing
プルル
ルル
Riiiiing
ルル
ルル
IT'S SEIMEI!! SEIMEI!!

Riiiiiiiing
SEIMEI IS...
NO...
Riiiiiiiiing
...CALLING ME!
IT'S TRUE!
HE CALLED BEFORE, JUST NOW! HE SAID HE'D CALL BACK!
Riiiiiiiing
Incoming Call
SEIMEI IS... DEAD.
Riiiiiiiiing

Riiiiiiiiiiing
Riiiiiiiiiiing
Seimei...
She says it's Seimei.
It can't be.
Riiiiiiiiing
I chose to believe you, Soubi.
Riiiiiiiiing
Seimei is dead.

......
AOYAGI RESIDENCE...
HOW FAITHFUL OF YOU...

I WONDER IF THEY'LL COME...
I'M SURE THEY WILL.
OUR JOB IS JUST TO DELAY THEM, RIGHT?
WE AREN'T GOING TO OVERDO IT, RIGHT?
HE HAS NO CHOICE.
OKAY.
...I'M GOING TO HAVE A QUIZ SOON...
...AT SCHOOL.
A TEST.
THAT'S A BIG DEAL.

SHALL I HELP YOU STUDY?
NO, NO, THAT'S OKAY.
THAT'S NOT WHAT I MEANT.
OH, REALLY? A QUIZ IS JUST MEMORIZATION, USUALLY.
WHEN I FINISH MY TEST... I WANT TO GO SHOPPING...
I WANT TO GO.
NO, I WON'T.
ギュ
?
WHICH IS IT?
WILL YOU GO ...
... WITH ME?
YOU'RE ASKING ME?!
YES.
WHAT DO YOU WANT TO BUY?
DO YOU WANT SHOPPING ADVICE? OH!
NO, DUMMY!
IS IT A PRESENT FOR A BOY?
I DON'T HAVE ANYTHING PARTICULAR IN MIND. IS THAT OKAY?! I DON'T HAVE ANYTHING IN MIND!!

I'M A "FIGHTER," ANYWAY, SO WHAT DOES IT MATTER?!
HE MAY BE YOUR "FELLOW" BUT I'M MIMURO'S FIGHTER!

IF-IF-IF...
...YOU GO SHOPPING W-W-WITH ME, WHAT'S THE BIG DEAL?
IT IS A BIG DEAL.

HE MAY NOT LOOK IT, MEI-CHAN, BUT NISEI IS VERY NASTY.
fu fu fu
I CAN'T SAY NO TO HIM.

HE ASKS ME DIRECTLY, LIKE, "SENPAI, PLEASE."
AND I CAN'T TURN DOWN REQUESTS LIKE THAT. I'M WEAK.
P--
P--
PLEASE?
THAT'S RIGHT, PLEASE.

PEOPLE WHO DON'T ASK, WHO SIMPLY DEMAND...
...I HAVE NO PROBLEM SAYING NO TO THEM.

SO WHY DON'T YOU TRY ASKING PROPERLY, MEI?

HM?

YOU'RE SUCH...

......

...A JERK.

YOU'RE A JERK, MIMURO.

NISEI CAN BE THAT WAY BECAUSE HE DOESN'T THINK ANYTHING OF YOU, MIMURO.

The Sacrifice Chapters
Chapter 17

RITSUKA...
YOU MUST BE COLD LIKE THAT. NO COAT.

MOTHER WAS MISTAKEN WHEN SHE SAID THE CALL WAS FROM SEIMEI.

OR SHE WAS DELUSIONAL.

SHE *IS* CRAZY, ISN'T SHE?

SOUBI!!

WHY ARE YOU ANGRY?
ANY WOMAN WHO WOULD ABUSE HER OWN CHILD IS CLEARLY OUT OF HER MIND.
SHE'S BETTER OFF DEAD.

SOUBI, DON'T EVER SAY THAT AGAIN!!
YOU DON'T KNOW ANYTHING ABOUT HER!
MOTHER IS... IT'S NOT THAT...
I CAN TELL BY LOOKING AT HER, THERE'S SOMETHING WRONG WITH HER.

THERE'S NOTHING WRONG WITH HER...!!
AH...
THEN YOU'RE FINE WITH THE WAY SHE TREATS YOU, RITSUKA?
...RITSUKA'S ABOUT TO CRY. WHAT SHOULD I DO?
SHUT UP.
I'M FINE...
...WITH IT, YES.
I'D LIKE TO SEE HIM CRY.
AS LONG AS SHE DOESN'T GET KILLED...
...LIKE SEIMEI. AS LONG AS SHE DOESN'T LEAVE ME.
AS LONG AS MOTHER IS AT HOME WITH ME, I'M HAPPY WITH THAT.

AS LONG AS SHE'S WITH YOU.. YOU'RE FIN WITH THAT?

ARE YOU A MASOCHIST?

OR...

...AN ANGEL?

I'M FINE.

RITSUKA IS...

LET'S GO.

...LOOKING FOR SOMETHING TO LOVE.

OKAY.

HE DESIRES AN OBJECT FOR THIS LOVE SO MUCH...

It's big.

...THAT WHEN HE THINKS HE'S FOUND IT, HE GIVES THAT PERSON ALL HE HAS.

But agreeing to love—to trust love's object unquestioningly—that, too, is insanity.

HELLO, SEIMEI?!
IT'S REALLY YOU, ISN'T IT, SEIMEI?
RITSUKA!
IT'S SEIMEI!!
THAT'S NOT POSSIBLE, MOTHER.
GIVE ME THE PHONE.
HELLO.
AOYAGI RITSUKA-KUN?
WHO IS THIS?
IT'S NOT SEIMEI!!

MOTHER. THIS IS...
...SOMEBODY I DON'T KNOW. WHY...
I'M SORRY TO CALL SO LATE, BUT WE'RE WAITING AT THE PARK IN DISTRICT 2.
WHA...
YOU SHOULD HURRY. WE DON'T LIKE TO WAIT.
YOU WANT TO KNOW ABOUT SEIMEI, DON'T YOU?
YOU...
WHO ARE YOU...?!
RITSUKA?
RIGHT?
IT REALLY WAS SEIMEI, WASN'T IT?!
MOTHER...

RIGHT
HE SAID HE WAS COMING HOME SOON, DIDN'T HE?
MOTHER...
ギコギコ
cree cree cree
AH!
MEI?
THEY'RE ... COMING!
THE ENEMY.
THIS IS...
...WOW.

WOW...
...YOU REALLY DID COME OUT AT THIS HOUR. WHAT A LITTLE DELINQUENT.

SO THAT'S AGATSUMA SOUBI!!

THAT'S A LITTLE HYPOCRITICAL, FROM SOMEONE WHO CALLED MY *HOME* AT THIS HOUR.
IF YOU'VE GOT BUSINESS WITH ME, LET'S GET IT OVER WITH.

SYSTEMS ON!
REQUESTING BATTLE!

WHOA.

YOU'RE JUST GOING TO JUMP IN HEADFIRST, MEI?

I WOULD HAVE LIKED TO TALK A BIT MORE.
ESPECIALLY SINCE RITSUKA-KUN IS SO CUTE IN THAT GIANT COAT.
THIS ISN'T MINE!!

...YOUR HANDS ARE COLD.

LET ME HOLD THEM.
THEN I'LL FIGHT FOR YOU, RITSUKA.

FOR YOU, MY RITSUKA...
...ALL COLD AND SOAKING WET.
THEN FIGHT.
FIGHT, AND MAKE THEM TELL EVERYTHING.
IF ANYONE TRIES TO HIDE ANYTHING FROM ME, TEAR HIM TO PIECES!!

THEN I'LL BEGIN.
OUR NAME IS LOVELESS.
WE ARE FEARLESS.
AND THAT'S OUR POWER... WE AREN'T AFRAID OF ANYTHING!!

Aoyagi
THE HUMAN BRAIN PROTECTS US FROM OUR SENSES.
IT ALLOWS US TO SEE WHAT IT WANTS US TO SEE, HEAR WHAT IT WANTS US TO HEAR.
IT DOESN'T LIKE DEFIED EXPECTATIONS. BUT THEN... HOW DO WE EVER KNOW WHAT'S REAL?
WHAT-EVER.
SYSTEMS ON.

I'M HOME.
MOTHER, I'M HOME.
IT'S ME, SEIMEI.

YOU...

WHO ARE YOU...?!

RITSUKA?

RIGHT?

IT REALLY WAS SEIMEI, WASN'T IT?

RIGHT?

MOTHER...

HE SAID HE WAS COMING HOME SOON, DIDN'T HE?

MOTH
RITSUKA. WHY DO YOU LOOK SO STRANGE?
UM.
UHH...
HE HUNG UP.
......
LET'S GO TO BED.

ARE THESE YOUR PAJAMAS?
YOU CAN GET DRESSED, RIGHT?
Nod
......
GO TO SLEEP, MOTHER.
I'LL SEE YOU TOMORROW.
GOOD NIGHT.

SEIMEI WILL SAVE ME. SEIMEI WILL HELP ME. SEIMEI WILL STOP ME.
SEIMEI WILL PROTECT RITSUKA FROM ME.
I'M GLAD.
I'M HOME.
!!
I'M HOME. IT'S ME, SEIMEI.
MOTHER.

SEIMEI!!
I'M HOME.
SEIMEI.
SEIMEI.
WHY WEREN'T YOU HOME EARLIER?
IT WAS A LIE, WASN'T IT? YOU WEREN'T DEAD!
I'M SORRY.
MOTHER.
I'M SORRY.
DON'T GO AWAY ANYMORE.
PLEASE SAVE RITSUKA.
LET ME LOOK AT YOU.
SEIMEI...
CALM DOWN.

MOTHER...
...YOU SEE, I...
I COULDN'T COME HOME BECAUSE OF RITSUKA.
...WHAT?
IF RITSUKA'S HERE, I CAN'T RETURN HOME.
WHAT... WHY?
DO YOU MEAN THAT RITSUKA NEEDS TO GO AWAY?
THAT'S RIGHT.
HE NEEDS TO GO.
WHAT SHOULD I DO?
SHOULD I LOCK RITSUKA UP?
HMM. NO.
THAT WON'T WORK.

THEN...

THEN...

SHALL I CHASE HIM AWAY...?

HMM.

THAT WON'T WORK EITHER...

ISN'T THERE ANY OTHER WAY? THINK HARD.

WHAT...

BUT WHAT SHOULD I DO...

RITSUKA NEEDS TO BE GONE, MOTHER.

The Sacrifice Chapters
Chapter 8
key
?

FENRI
....

I'M SURE YOU ALREADY KNOW THIS, MEI...
...BUT I'M NOT GOING TO USE ANY DEFENSE.
!

MIMURO...

BECAUSE THAT'S OUR STYLE. RIGHT?

BATTLING ALL THESE LITTLE KIDS LATELY IS MAKING ME FEEL LIKE SUCH A VILLAIN.
AND THEY JUST KEEP COMING.
HERE WE GO AGAIN.
BE SERIOUS!

A SPELL OF BINDING!
!
AGH...
...HERE IT COMES!
MIMURO.
DON'T WORRY.

NEXT WE ATTACK...
N-NO.
WE'RE...
...GOING TO DEFEND.
WHAAAT?
HEY, WAIT, MEI- DON'T MAKE DECISIONS ON YOUR OWN...
MISTER DUCK!
PLEASE COME OUT!!
WAH!
WAH! WHAT THE HECK IS THAT?!
A FIGHTER UNIT WHO HASN'T BEEN CON-TROLLED YET.

MEIIII.

What is this?

DUCKS ARE CUTE!!

IN A SPELL BATTLE, THE FIGHTER CONJURES AN IMAGE IN HIS MIND AND CREATES IT BY SPEAKING IT IN WORDS. THE IMAGE-INTO-WORD IS WHAT MANIFESTS REAL POWER.

THE FASTER AND MORE VARIED THE CONNECTIONS, THE MORE POWERFUL THE ATTACK.

IN THE CASE OF THIS CHILD, HER LIMITED VOCABULARY HOLDS BACK HER POWER.

BUT THE IMAGES ARE STRONG...

SHE MIGHT BE GOOD.

GOOD...? ...REALLY?
SHE DOESN'T SEEM TO BE ANY OLDER THAN I AM.
DON'T WORRY ABOUT ME...
B-BE...
BE QUIET, MIMURO! I'M CONCEN-TRATING.
LEAVES...
BECOME BLADES, AND SLICE THE ENEMY.
LEAVES...
PIERCE THE ENEMY LIKE ARROWS.
TENS.
HUNDREDS.
THOUSANDS.
GO!

NO!
A STEEL CAGE TO PROTECT MIMURO!
APPEAR!!
!!

RITSUKA. THERE.
WHAT DOES THAT LOOK LIKE TO YOU?
MEI, LISTEN TO ME.
OR ELSE I CAN'T GIVE YOU MY POWER.
I KNOW!!
WHAT...
...A BOX...A CUBE?
NO.
IT'S A JUNGLE GYM.
RIGHT. THIS CHILD...
SHE'S USING THE OBJECTS AROUND HER TO ENHANCE HER IMAGERY.

IT'S VERY DIFFICULT TO CONSTRUCT A POWERFUL IMAGE QUICKLY ENOUGH, ESPECIALLY IN THE STRESS OF BATTLE.
PREPARING THINGS AROUND YOU TO TRIGGER IMAGES MORE EASILY IS A SOLID METHOD.
THIS PARK IS A GOOD PLACE FOR A CHILD TO BATTLE.
THE SPELLS SHE INVOKES THIS WAY ARE SIMPLE AND FAST.
HER EXPERIENCE LEVELS SEEM LOW, BUT THAT MEANS SHE'S DOING A LOT OF THIS BY INSTINCT. SO SHE HAS POTENTIAL.
BUT SHE MAY BE A POOR STUDENT--SHE DOESN'T HAVE THE BASICS DOWN.
...YOU MEAN BECAUSE THEY'RE ARGUING?
THAT'S RIGHT.
THE FIGHTER UNIT OBEYS.
THAT'S THE ONLY THING HE CAN DO.
UNLESS THE TWO ARE STRONGLY BONDED, THEY CANNOT BECOME POWERFUL.

ARE WE BONDED?

OF COURSE.

THEN...

...IF YOU UNDERSTAND MY FEELINGS, GO AHEAD AND DO IT.

I DO UNDERSTAND.

YOU WANT THIS TO END QUICKLY, DON'T YOU, RITSUKA?

STRAINS OF NEGATIVE POWER GATHER TOGETHER. TAKE FORM. DESTROY THE ENEMIES' CAGED BODIES IN ONE BLOW!!

HERE IT COMES.

ISN'T THERE SOME WAY TO ATTACK WHILE DEFENDING?!

The Sacrifice Chapters
Chapter 9

AHH.
THEIR DEFENSE BOUNCED BACK THE ATTACK.
WE DID IT?!
Heh!
SHE'S LEARNING, BUT...
...THIS IS WEAK.

AW...
GYAAAAH!

HEY!
KNOCK IT OFF!
ぱし

GYaaaaH!
STOP IT! CREEP!!

MY MASTER TOLD ME TO CRUSH YOU, AND I OBEYED.
YOU SHOULD LISTEN TO YOUR MASTER MORE OFTEN, YOUNG LADY.
SHUT UP! IT'S NONE OF YOUR BUSINESS!!
HE'S GOT A POINT, THOUGH.

BROTHER, MAYBE YOU DON'T KNOW ENOUGH ABOUT HER YET.
My hat!
DON'T TOUCH IT! GERMS!!

WHAAT?
WE LOST.
TCH.
WHAT ABOUT SEIMEI?!

I DON'T KNOW.
WHO'S SEIMEI?

DON'T PLAY DUMB. AOYAGI SEIMEI.
YOU KNOW SOMETHING, DON'T YOU?!
AOYAGI?
OH.

I HAD LUNCH WITH HIM LAST WEEK.
THAT'S ALL.

LAST WEEK...
...LUNCH...?

REALLY...?

WHAT'S WITH YOU?

I HAVE NO REASON TO LIE NOW... WE LOST.

LAST WEEK... I THINK IT WAS THURSDAY. A FRIEND BROUGHT HIM, AND THE THREE OF US WENT TO SHIBUYA.

WAS...

...THAT REALLY SEIMEI...?

THAT'S WHAT HE CALLED HIMSELF. HE WAS TALL WITH BLACK HAIR.

HE HAD SPLENDID EARS AND A TAIL, AND WAS VERY POLITE.

HE'S 17. YOUNGER THAN ME.

LET'S GO HOME, SOUBI...!!

NICE WORK. BYE-BYE.

phew
MIMURO, ARE YOU ALL RIGHT?!

I'M FINE.
BUT WHY WON'T YOU LISTEN TO ME?
OWWWWWW!!

BUT...
I DON'T LIKE YOUR STRATEGY, MIMURO.

MEI.
OUR NAME IS FEARLESS.
YEAH...
WE DECIDED WE'D NEVER BE AFRAID OF HURTING EACH OTHER.
THAT WE'D NEVER WORRY ABOUT LOSING EACH OTHER. THAT'S FREEDOM, RIGHT?
YES...
THEN WHY WON'T YOU LISTEN TO ME?

HE WAS CUTE, WASN'T HE?
HM?
MI--
MI--
MIMURO...
HERE'S YOUR HAT.
WHY DO YOU ALWAYS HIDE YOUR HAIR, MEI?

YOU LIE, YOU LIE!
snff
YOU LIKE BOYS, MIMURO. YOU'RE GAY!

UH.
MEI?

IF NOT, THEN WHY...

...AH. IF YOU'RE TALKING ABOUT NISEI, THAT'S A SPECIAL CASE.
AND I DON'T LIKE HIM THAT WAY.
Graah!
NOOOOOOO!

NGH... MNNN...
waahh!!
I DON'T WANT TO HEAR WHAT HE LIKES. THAT SOMEONE IS SPECIAL.
IF HE LIKES GIRLS, WHY DOESN'T HE LIKE ME?

...WHY DON'T YOU LET YOUR HAIR DOWN?
YOU LOOK CUTER THAT WAY.
NO!
Graaah!
Graaah!
DON'T SAY I'M CUTE!
NOT WHEN YOU SAID NISEI AND RITSUKA ARE CUTE, TOO!
......
I HATE YOU, MIMURO! I HATE YOU!

RITSUKA.

DO YOU BELIEV THEM?
OR NOT?
WHAT THEY SAID.
WHAT I SAID.

DO YOU BELIEVE?
SOUBI.

ARE YOU AFRAID?
BUT THAT GUY DIDN'T SEEM TO KNOW ANYTHING.
THAT'S WHY I FELT HE WAS TELLING THE TRUTH.
I BELIEVE YOU.
SOMETHING IS HAPPENING SOMEWHERE, AND YOU DON'T KNOW ABOUT IT, AND I DON'T KNOW ABOUT IT.
ARE YOU AFRAID?
I'M NOT AFRAID. BECAUSE I HAVE YOU, RITSUKA.
THEN DON'T EVER ASK ME IF I BELIEVE YOU AGAIN!
IT'S COWARDLY!!

DON'T KEEP ASKING ME OVER AND OVER! KNOW IT!

WHY DON'T YOU BELIEVE ME?!

......
I DO.

YOU ANSWERED LATE!
YES, SIR!
ALL RIGHT!

LISTEN, SOUBI, PLEASE.

DON'T ASK ME ANYTHING MORE.

IT MAKES ME FEEL CHOKED ...

...LIKE THERE'S A KNIFE TO MY THROAT.

DON'T ASK ME. JUST KNOW. JUST KNOW.

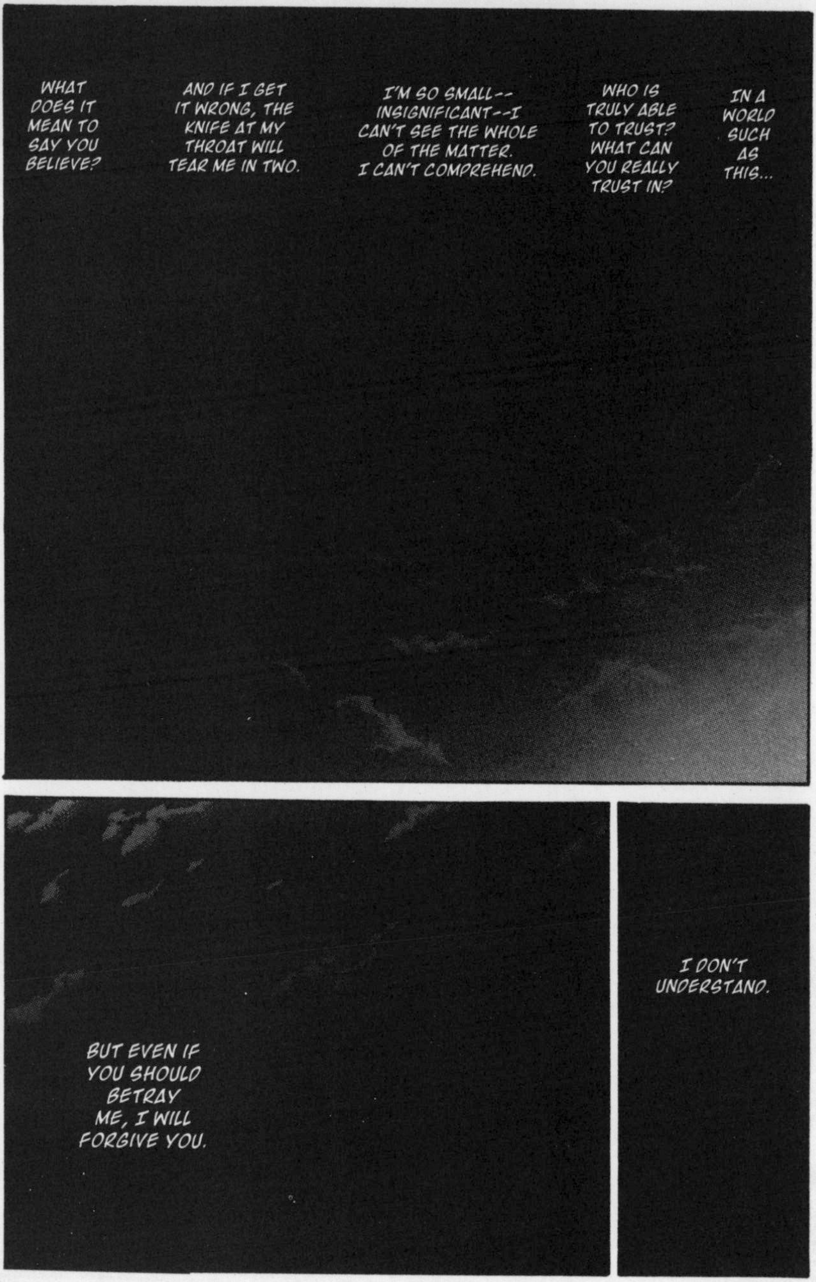

WHAT DOES IT MEAN TO SAY YOU BELIEVE?

AND IF I GET IT WRONG, THE KNIFE AT MY THROAT WILL TEAR ME IN TWO.

I'M SO SMALL--INSIGNIFICANT--I CAN'T SEE THE WHOLE OF THE MATTER. I CAN'T COMPREHEND.

WHO IS TRULY ABLE TO TRUST? WHAT CAN YOU REALLY TRUST IN?

IN A WORLD SUCH AS THIS...

BUT EVEN IF YOU SHOULD BETRAY ME, I WILL FORGIVE YOU.

I DON'T UNDERSTAND.

THAT'S WHAT KNOWING IS.
THAT'S WHAT IT MEANS TO BELIEVE.
SEIMEI.
I DON'T... UNDER-STAND.
I THOUGHT ABOUT IT.
I SEE... THEN, SHALL I JUST TELL YOU?
YES! TELL ME!!
WHY DON'T YOU KILL RITSUKA?

I THINK THAT WOULD BE PERFECT.
...WHAT...?

YOU'RE SPILLING YOUR PILLS, MOTHER. TAKE THEM ALL, LIKE A GOOD GIRL.
YES...
TAKE THEM AND YOU'LL FEEL BETTER.
MMN...

HM...
WHAT...
WHAT DID YOU JUST SAY?
DO WHAT WITH RITSUKA?

LISTEN, MOM.
IF RITSUKA IS HERE, THEN I CAN'T COME BACK HOME. THAT'S WHY WE SHOULD GET RID OF RITSUKA.
SOON RITSUKA WILL COME THROUGH THE DOOR.
YOU CAN GRAB HIM BY THE NECK... AND STRANGLE HIM.

RITSUKA'S...
...NECK?
UNTIL HE STOPS BREATHING. YOU HAVE TO BE SURE TO CRUSH HIS WINDPIPE.
I DON'T WANT THAT.
I DON'T WANT RITSUKA TO BE GONE.

I WANT YOU BOTH!!
BOTH YOU AND RITSUKA ARE MINE!!
THEN ...
I SUPPOSE IT REALLY CAN'T BE HELPED.
DON'T GO, SEIMEI!
PLEASE!
BUT YOU SAID YOU'D RATHER HAVE RITSUKA.
NO, I WANT BOTH!
THAT'S NOT FAIR.
IT IS FAIR! PLEASE!
I WON'T LET YOU GO...
......

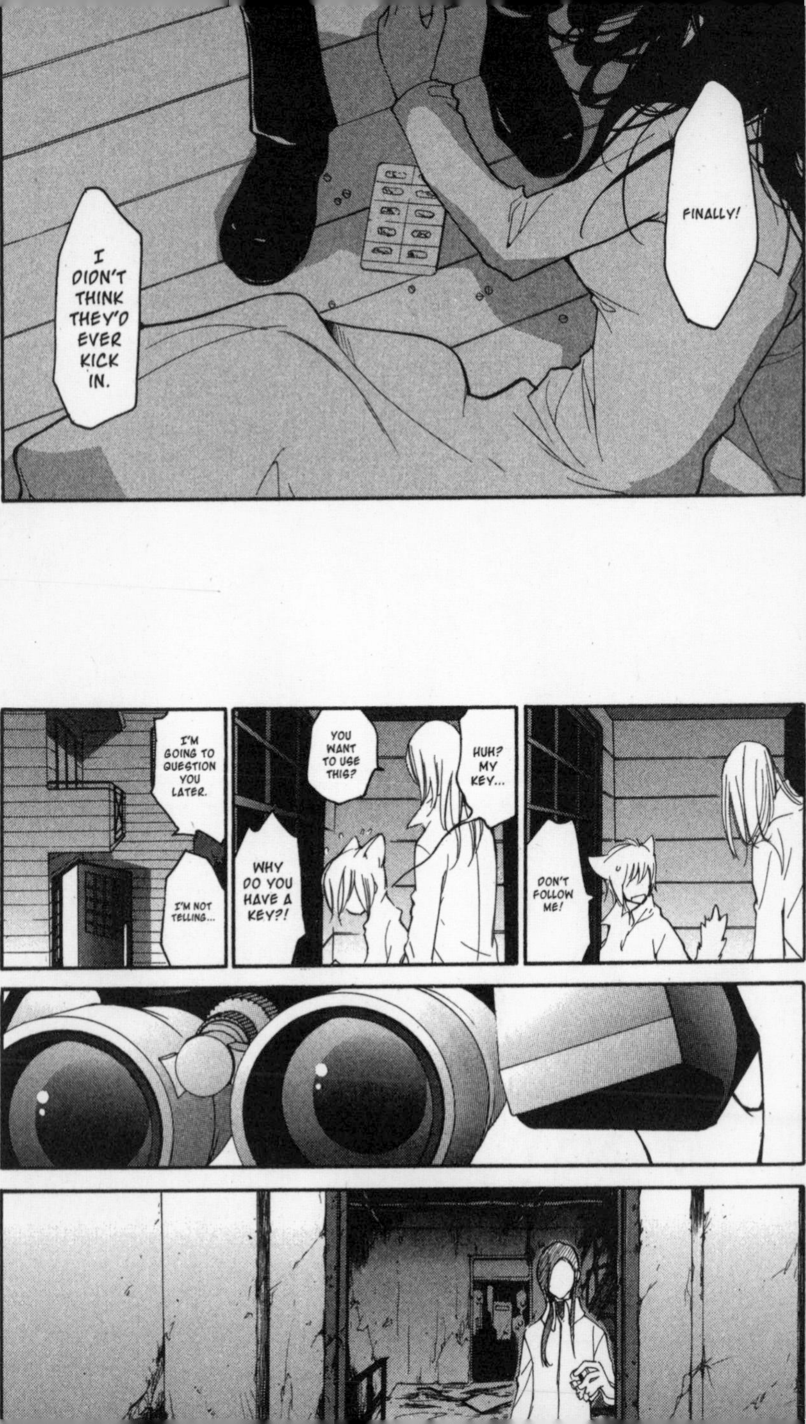

FINALLY!

I DIDN'T THINK THEY'D EVER KICK IN.

HUH? MY KEY...

DON'T FOLLOW ME!

YOU WANT TO USE THIS?

WHY DO YOU HAVE A KEY?!

I'M GOING TO QUESTION YOU LATER.

I'M NOT TELLING...

THIS IS...
...AKAME.

AH HA HA...
IT SEEMS THAT IT DIDN'T WORK.
I HAD A FEELING IT WOULD FAIL...

...YES, I HAD MIMURO-SAN'S HELP.
THAT'S RIGHT.
WE ATE LUNCH TOGETHER LAST THURSDAY, REMEMBER?
THOSE TWO DON'T BELONG TO ANYONE.
BUT THAT WOMAN IS A TERROR.

SHE REJECTED MY SUGGESTION TO STRANGLE HIM. SHAME. THAT WAS A FUN ONE.
BUT SHE'S REALLY DRUGGED, SO HE'LL BE IN FOR A SHOCK WHEN HE GETS HOME.
IT ISN'T ENOUGH. BUT IT'S... A LIGHT AMUSEMENT.

SHE'S SUCH A GREEDY COW. IT ACTUALLY MADE ME SICK.
SHE SAYS SHE WANTS BOTH RITSUKA AND SEIMEI.
YEAH.

SHE'S ALWAYS BEEN LIKE THAT.
OH?

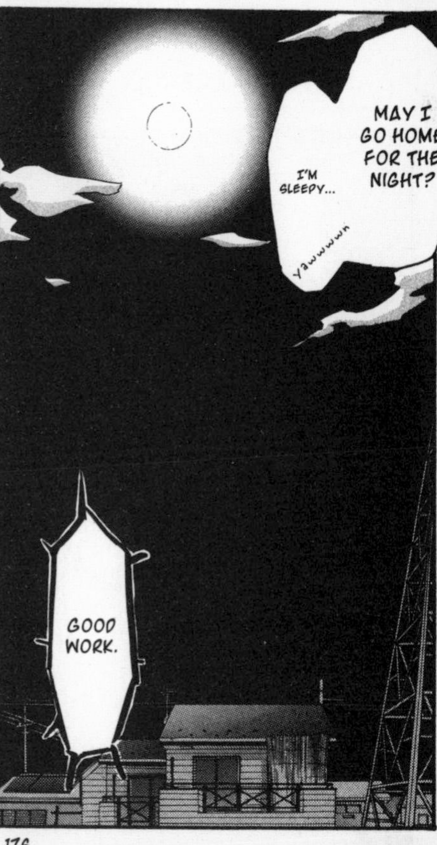
MAY I GO HOME FOR THE NIGHT?
I'M SLEEPY...
yawwwwn
GOOD WORK.

GOOD NIGHT, NISEI.
GOOD NIGHT, SEIMEI.
TALK TO YOU TOMORROW.

MOTHER!

MOTHER, WHAT HAP-PENED?
GET A HOLD OF YOUR-SELF.
SHE'S SLEEPING.
AH...
IF SHE'S ON PILLS, SHE WON'T WAKE UP THAT EASILY.

SHE HAS LOTS OF SLEEPING PILLS, DOESN'T SHE?

......

SHALL I CARRY HER TO HER BED?

YOU CAN'T DO IT ALONE, RITSUKA.

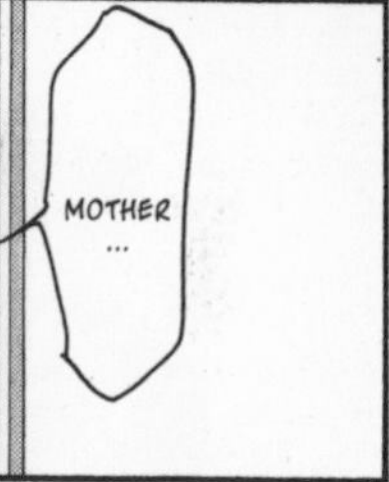
MOTHER ...

SHE TOOK THIS MANY PILLS...?!

I DON'T LIKE PEOPLE WHO RELY ON DRUGS.
SHE'S NOT LIKE THAT.

IT'S WEAK.
I DON'T LIKE WEAK PEOPLE.

SOME-ONE LIKE THAT...

...WELL, SHE'S JUST LIKE ME.

AND THAT'S NO FUN AT ALL.

I DON'T KNOW ABOUT YOU, BUT MOTHER'S NOT WEAK!

SHE ONLY TAKES WHAT SHE NEEDS WHEN SHE NEEDS IT.

ENOUGH TO FALL ASLEEP AT THE FRONT DOOR IN THE MIDDLE OF THE NIGHT IN WINTER?

That's dangerous.

NOT EVERYTHING IN THIS WORLD IS DONE ON PURPOSE. PEOPLE MAKE MISTAKES!

AND WHY DO YOU HAVE A KEY TO MY HOUSE?

NEVER MIND.

I ALREADY KNOW.

MAYBE YOU MADE A SPARE KEY.
IT'S SOMETHING YOU'D DO. BUT IT'S NOT WHAT YOU DID DO.
YOU GOT IT FROM SEIMEI.
......
BUT WE MOVED TO THIS HOUSE AFTER SEIMEI DIED.
SO THERE'S NO WAY SEIMEI COULD HAVE GIVEN YOU THAT KEY.
UNLESS ...
...SEIMEI'S ALIVE.

Ritsuka's Day
Chirp chirp
GOOD MORNING. IT'S TIME FOR THE 7 O'CLOCK NEWS.
YOUR TOAST'S READY, RITSUKA.
WHAT DO YOU WANT ON IT?
ボケー
ping
MMM... CHEESE AND HONEY...
APRIL 4TH, TODAY IS SEIMEI.

HUH?
THE GRASS AND TREES ARE BUDDING. SPRING'S FINALLY ARRIVED.
SEIMEI!!
TODAY'S SEIMEI!! DID YOU KNOW?
THIS MARKS THE START OF THE THIRD MONTH OF TWENTY-FOUR IN THE LUNAR-SOLAR CALENDAR.
YEAH.
WE WERE NAMED AFTER THE MONTHS IN THE TRADITIONAL CALENDAR.
OH.
WE?
SO THAT MEANS...
THERE'S A DAY FOR RITSUKA, TOO.
WOW. I WONDER WHEN THAT IS.
I THINK IT'S AROUND MAY 5TH. IT VARIES DEPENDING ON THE YEAR.

In 2005, seimei was April 5, rikka was May 5.

YOUR NAME IS RITSUKA, SO IT'S A BIT DIFFERENT FROM RIKKA.
ズー…
BUT MOM HAD "RIKKA" IN MIND WHEN SHE NAMED YOU.
WHAT DAY IS RIKKA?
IT'S THE FIRST DAY OF SUMMER.

THE FIRST DAY OF SUMMER?
HUH?

BUT WAIT A MINUTE. I WAS BORN ON DECEMBER 21.
That's the middle of winter.
WHY?
YUP!

AND I WAS BORN ON NOVEMBER 14, AND CALLED SEIMEI.
WHY DO YOU THINK THAT IS?
IS THERE A REASON?
THERE IS.

SINCE YOU WERE BORN ON DECEMBER 21, YOU SHOULD BE "TOJI," FOR THE WINTER SOLSTICE.
I KINDA DON'T LIKE THAT.
SO WHY? WHY?
WHAT KIND OF REASON?
YOU WANT TO KNOW?
I WANT TO KNO-OOOOW!
THE ANSWER IS WRITTEN IN MOTHER'S DIARY.
HUH?!
WHOSE?
OUR MOTHER WROTE IT...
WHAT?
...IN HER DIARY.
WHAAA-AAAT?
SEIMEI, YOU READ MOM'S DIARY?
WHO KNOWS? WHAT DO YOU THINK?

WHAT DO YOU MEAN, WHAT DO I THINK?
BUT...
YOU MUST HAVE READ IT.
SEIMEI, YOU'RE BAD.
I'M BAD?
WHY?
YOU'RE NOT SUPPOSED TO READ OTHER PEOPLE'S DIARIES.
YOU'RE NOT INTRIGUED, RITSUKA?
I AM! BUT THAT'S DIFFERENT.
I'M NOT BAD.
IT'S HER FAULT FOR WRITING IT.
SO IF YOU READ IT, YOU'RE NOT AT FAULT, RITSUKA.

ONCE HER SECRET WAS CONFIDED TO PAPER...
IT'S HER FAULT FOR LEAVING A SECRET WHERE OTHERS COULD FIND IT.
...THAT SECRET BEGAN TO BREAK OPEN.
RITSUKA.
IF YOU REALLY WANT TO PROTECT A SECRET, YOU CAN'T LEAVE IT IN ANY TANGIBLE FORM.
YOU CAN'T EVEN SAY, "I'VE GOT A SECRET." A REAL SECRET DOESN'T EXIST.

RIGHT?
Smile
I LOVE SEIMEI. THAT'S THE TRUTH.
...EVEN SO...
I WOULDN'T WANT SOMEBODY TO LOOK THROUGH MY DIARY WITHOUT MY PERMISSION.
BUT I SOMETIMES THINK THAT SOMETHING ISN'T RIGHT... EVEN THOUGH I CAN'T EXPLAIN WHAT IT IS.
I DON'T DO THINGS TO OTHERS THAT I WOULDN'T WANT DONE TO MYSELF.
WHY ARE YOU LOOKING AWAY?
I KNOW WHY.
THE TRUTH IS, YOU'RE AFRAID OF ME. AREN'T YOU, RITSUKA?
NO!
I...
I'M NOT AFRAID. I LOVE YOU!!

TODAY IS DECEMBER 21--TOJI. IT'S GOTTEN COLD.
OOPS, OH... I NODDED OFF.
EVERYONE SHOULD TAKE A HOT YUZU CITRUS BATH, AND EAT PUMPKINS.
I HAVE TO GO.
AND NOW FOR TODAY'S NEWS...
YOU SEE, SEIMEI, I...
...I WANT TO ASK MOM ONE DAY, AND I WANT HER TO TELL ME.
WANTING HER TO GIVE HER CONFIDENCE FREELY... THAT KEEPS HER SECRET SAFE.
I'M GOING.

I DON'T WANT TO KNOW HER SECRET. NOT IF SHE WANTS TO HIDE IT.
OH.
TODAY'S DECEMBER 21.
YOU SEE, I LIKE MY NAME. THIS NAME THAT MY MOTHER GAVE ME.
SO NOW I'M 12 YEARS OLD.
I'M GLAD I WASN'T NAMED TOJI...
Aoyagi Ritsuka, born December 21.

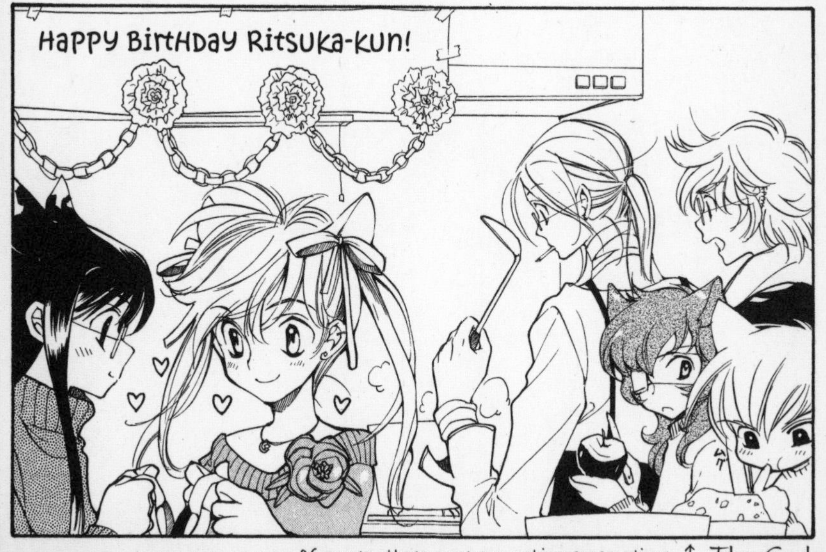

Of course, these guys are making preparations. ↑ The End

Backstage Stories Loveless
VOLUME 5 CAME OUT EARLIER THAN EXPECTED.
YOU THINK? IT'S BEEN 8 MONTHS, SO NOT REALLY.
Not cute at all!
← Me
Editor →
We don't seem to get along very well.
Uh-huh.
Well, let's talk about upcoming scenarios.
All right.
Side view
Side view
How about Seimei is being harbored by a 30-year-old single OL, whaddaya think?!
Flutter
That's good!
giggle
Whaaaat? That's totally uncool!
It is cool, idiot!
It makes him look pitiful!
I mean, hey, is Seimei even alive?!
What?!
COOLNESS!
It seems our perceptions of "coolness" are not in sync.
It's cool to be harbored by an older woman!
I dunno. I think a guy like that is pitiful.
Hmph
Such distance between our souls!
So we dumped that idea.
Mmmm. I thought it was a good idea, dammit. That's the problem with guys...
Now then, on to the subject of the anime.
THE VOICE TALENT HAS BEEN CAST.
OH REALLY, LET ME SEE PLEASE.
SEIMEI...
...IS BEING PLAYED BY YAKUSHOMARU-SAMA!!
Ritsuka Played by Minakawa Junko-san
Soubi Played by Ogawa Katsuyuki-san
Yuiko Played by Naota Yoshina-san
It's wonderful!!

The animation adaptation is wholly due to all my wonderful readers. Thank you very much!! I've had my work animated before, but this is my first one for TV, and the whole experience was different than the last time. I'll try my hardest not to get in the way.
I've been blessed with such a great staff, I almost feel unworthy of being treated so well.

I'm going to try to reciprocate everyone's hard work.
Please enjoy!!

You can check for updates on the series at:
www.tokyopop.com

Kouga Yun official website
www.kokonoe.com

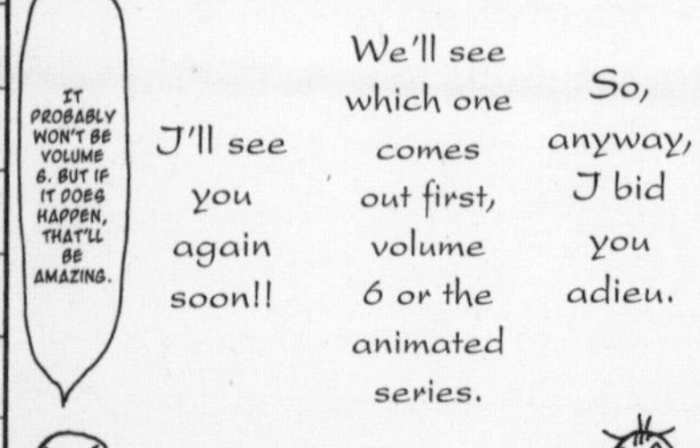

The End

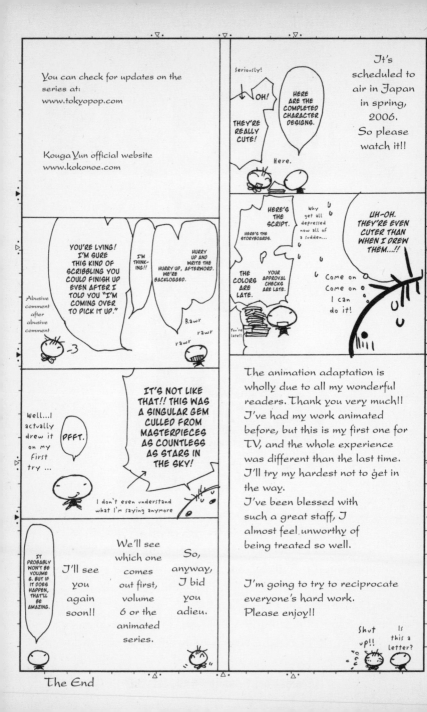

In The Next Volume of

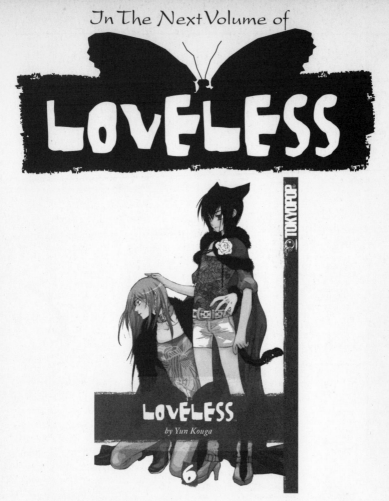

LOVELESS

The secret behind of Seimei's disappearance and apparent death begins to be unveiled, and the consequences are devastating to both Ritsuka and Soubi. Nisei privately reveals an even more shocking truth to Soubi, which shakes the Fighter to the core, and Misaki's abuse of Ritsuka escalates to the point where it can no longer be ignored by those around him. But a second meeting with Ritsu-sensei may send Ritsuka down a new path to find his destiny!

Loveless Vol. 6 Available August 2007

Lord Byron, writing about the multitudes contained in the human personality in his poem *Don Juan*, resigned himself, after a fashion, by stating: "I almost think that the same skin/For one without—has two or three within." Neuroscience would answer that couplet with dual brain theory, which states that each of the two separate hemispheres of the human brain works independently, and that one side (the artistic, moody right brain, for example) often dominates the other (the logical, verbal left brain).

Each character in Yun Kouga's *Loveless* doesn't stop at two or three, but contains a chorus of personalities—conflicting traits and shifting beliefs serve to keep her readers on their toes and the stories fresh. Beyond that, she says a great deal about the self and its relationships. First, the two sides of one being theme is built into the structure of the magic in the series. In the spell battles, one name ("Fearless" for example) has two parts—a Fighter and a Sacrifice. Opposites. Often in life, and always in *Loveless*, a thing is itself and its opposite— Ritsuka and Seimei are even named after seasons of the year opposite to the ones in which they were born.

Kouga also presents issues of gender (always fluid in the world of *Loveless*), and how looks can be deceiving—delicate-looking Nisei is a tough, sadistic male. "He may not look it," Miumuro warns Mei, "but Nisei is very nasty." Boyish Mei, hair hidden under a baseball cap, is something of a closet girly-girl. But she's a "shrewd kid"—she adds up a person's qualities before pronouncing that she "likes" or "hates" them. And Kouga often plays with us. When Ritsuka's online character is asked if he satisfies Soubi, he quickly ripostes with, "His voice is sore from screaming with pleasure." It's not until the next page that we find that it's Soubi giving dialogue for Ritsuka. "You've ruined my persona!" cries Ritsuka, as he clings to his identity fiercely, unable to give in to the changes that growing up inflicts on an ego.

Volume five centers around Ritsuka's quest to stay up all night—a nocturnal self to counter his diurnal "normal" life—to play an online game, hoping to find members of Septimal Moon and discover who murdered his brother, and why. The online world adds another layer of masks to obscure and reveal "real" personality traits. But instead of confronting Seimei's killers, Ritsuka confronts everything he ever thought was true about his brother—everything that made Seimei who he was.

Ritsuka's Seimei is a physical character—a tickling, joking, wrestling older brother, who doesn't hesitate to dress wounds and lavish affection on Ritsuka. Seven says this can't be Seimei. Her Seimei—Septimal Moon's Seimei—was extremely obsessive compulsive, didn't like to be touched by other people, wouldn't eat in front of others, and would never think of sleeping in the same bed as someone else. "He was calm and gentle, sure," Seven agrees. "But then, that isn't normal, either."

Soubi's Seimei, in contrast, was a harsh master: "You could sit outside his door a thousand years, and Seimei still wouldn't talk to you." Like the man in Kafka's "Before the Law," who waits his entire life for permission to enter a door from a gatekeeper, we are to infer that Soubi spent a lot of his time with Seimei just waiting—for direction, for acknowledgment, for love. When Yoji doesn't understand the subtleties of the relationship, thinking that since Seimei's dead, Soubi's now free, Soubi—who wants anything but freedom—sets him straight. "This is Seimei's arm…these are Seimei's legs…Even if Seimei isn't here, his orders are carried out." Soubi makes the metaphor flesh by tossing the recalcitrant Yoji out into the cold. "That's what it means to be dominated," Soubi says, with a bitter pride in his position. Now the man who can't enter the gates has become the gatekeeper, and Soubi stands guard, saying, "No one who harms Ritsuka may enter." Soubi is his own master, and his own slave. His arms and legs are Seimei's, Seimei's will is his own.

If Seimei isn't dead, whose was the charred body the police identified by dental records? Another "version" of Seimei? Some other body forced to play the role? As if the possibility of Seimei's being alive wasn't enough to shatter Ritsuka's "idea" of him, he is then presented as a criminal condemned to death, a "sinner." And Soubi, says Seven, knows all.

But Ritsuka can't, and doesn't accept it. He believes Soubi, he believes that Seimei is dead. For while Ritsuka can't accept that he is both the boy he was two years ago and the Ritsuka he is now, he has no problem integrating Seimei's personalities: "Seimei is just Seimei… there was only one." It "doesn't hurt" him to find out that Seimei had another side. His love for his brother, whoever his brother may have been, is the only thing that is important to him, unifying his own fractured identity, and melding the disparate stories of his brother's true nature into a single whole.

~Christine Boylan

SAKURA TAISEN

BY OHJI HIROI, IKKU MASA AND KOSUKE FUJISHIMA

I really, really like this series. I'm a sucker for steampunk-type stories, and 1920s Japanese fashion, and throw in demon invaders, robot battles and references to Japanese popular theater? Sold! There's lots of fun tidbits for the clever reader to pick up in this series (all the characters have flower names, for one, and the fact that all the Floral Assault divisions are named after branches of the Takarazuka Review, Japan's sensational all-female theater troupe!), but the consistently stylish and clean art will appeal even to the most casual fan.

~Lillian Diaz-Przybyl, Editor

BATTLE ROYALE

BY KOUSHUN TAKAMI AND MASAYUKI TAGUCHI

As far as cautionary tales go, you couldn't get any timelier than *Battle Royale*. Telling the bleak story of a class of middle school students who are forced to fight each other to the death on national television, Koushun Takami and Masayuki Taguchi have created a dark satire that's sickening, yet undeniably exciting as well. And if we have that reaction reading it, it becomes alarmingly clear how the students could so easily be swayed into doing it.

~Tim Beedle, Editor

ANGEL CUP

BY JAE-HO YOUN

Who's the newest bouncing broad that bends it like Beckam better than Braz—er, you get the idea? So-jin of the hit Korean manhwa, *Angel Cup!* She and her misfit team of athletic amazoness tear up the soccer field, whether it's to face up against the boys' team, or wear their ribbons with pride against a rival high school. While the feminist in me cheers for So-jin and the gang, the more perverted side of me drools buckets over the sexy bust-shots and scandalous camera angles... But from any and every angle, *Angel Cup* will be sure to tantalize the soccer fan in you... or perv. Whichever!

~Katherine Schilling, Jr. Editor

GOOD WITCH OF THE WEST

BY NORIKO OGIWARA AND HARUHIKO MOMOKAWA

For any dreamers who ever wanted more out of a fairytale, indulge yourself with *Good Witch*. Although there's lots of familiar territory fairytale-wise—peasant girl learns she's a princess—you'll be surprised as Firiel Dee's enemies turn out to be as diverse as religious fanaticism, evil finishing school student councils and dinosaurs. This touching, sophisticated tale will pull at your heartstrings while astounding you with breathtaking art. *Good Witch* has big shoes to fill, and it takes off running.

~Hope Donovan, Jr. Editor

STOP!

This is the back of the book. You wouldn't want to spoil a great ending!

This book is printed "manga-style," in the authentic Japanese right-to-left format. Since none of the artwork has been flipped or altered, readers get to experience the story just as the creator intended. You've been asking for it, so TOKYOPOP® delivered: authentic, hot-off-the-press, and far more fun!

DIRECTIONS

If this is your first time reading manga-style, here's a quick guide to help you understand how it works.

It's easy... just start in the top right panel and follow the numbers. Have fun, and look for more 100% authentic manga from TOKYOPOP®!